FARMERS

BY EMMA LESS

AMICUS READERS ● AMICUS INK

amicus
readers

Amicus Readers and Amicus Ink are imprints of Amicus
P.O. Box 1329, Mankato, MN 56002
www.amicuspublishing.us

Cataloging-in-Publication Data is on file with the Library of Congress.
ISBN 978-1-68151-294-5 (library binding)
ISBN 978-1-68152-276-0 (paperback)
ISBN 978-1-68151-356-0 (eBook)

Editor: Valerie Bodden
Designer: Patty Kelley

Photo Credits:
Cover: Jenoche/iStock.com
Inside: Dreamstime.com: Goodluz 4, Phaisit Jrienbhasaworn 6, Alongkorn Sumalee 13, Bjorn Heller 16TR, Giovanni Triganni 16TL, Harun 16B. Shutterstock: Monkey Business Images 3, 15, TfoxFoto 8, Goran Bogicevic 10.

Printed in China.

HC 10 9 8 7 6 5 4 3 2 1
PB 10 9 8 7 6 5 4 3 2 1

Farmers grow good food.
Ann meets some farmers.

This farmer grows wheat. Bread is made from wheat.

Here's a big
field of corn.

The farmer rides
in a tractor.
The tractor cuts
down the corn.

Some farmers
raise chickens.
Beth and Amy feed
the chickens seeds.

Farmers milk their cows. They clean up after the cows.

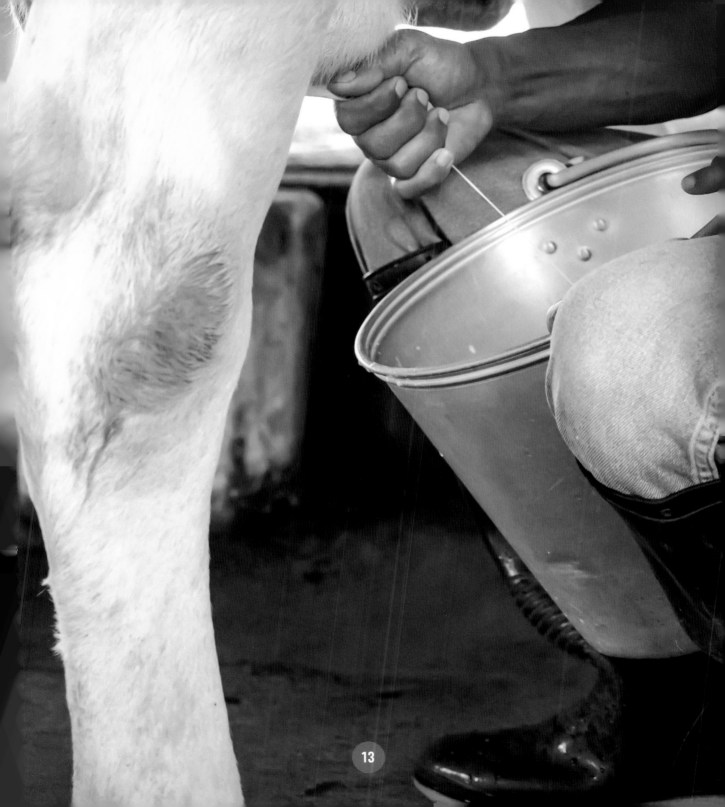

Look at all the
food from farms.
Dig in, Hope!

SEEN ON A FARM

hay

tractor

cow